STUD

THE PROMISE OF
THE FUTURE

Cornelis P. Venema

THE BANNER OF TRUTH TRUST

THE BANNER OF TRUTH TRUST
3 Murrayfield Road, Edinburgh EH12 6EL, UK
PO Box 621, Carlisle, PA 17013, USA

*

© The Banner of Truth Trust 2009

ISBN-13: 978 1 84871 025 2

*

Typeset in 10.5/14 pt Sabon Oldstyle Figures at
The Banner of Truth Trust, Edinburgh.
Printed in the USA by
VersaPress, Inc.,
East Peoria, IL.

*

The page numbers in this Study Guide
follow those in
Cornelis P. Venema,
The Promise of the Future
(Edinburgh: Banner of Truth, 2000)

PART ONE:
THE FUTURE IS NOW

CHAPTER 1:
'HOPE NURTURED BY THE WORD'
PAGES 3-11

1. How can we account for the many differing interpretations among Christians with regard to the end times?

2. What's the most important thing to remember when approaching the subject of the end times?

3. How can we best avoid disorientation about the future?

4. Will 'Paradise lost' become simply 'Paradise regained'? Why or why not? Explore how the original circumstances in Paradise compare with the new heavens and new earth in Revelation 22.

5. What characterizes the believer's expectation for the future?

6. What do you think it is about contemporary culture that gives us such a keen interest in the future? In what ways does our culture manifest an interest in the future?

7. As Christians, how can we ensure that we avoid an unhealthy speculation about the future?

8. How does the fact that Christ is Lord over history affect the way we view not only the past, but especially the future?

9. What is the difference between the way the Bible foretells the future and the modern practice of fortune telling (e.g. palm reading, fortunes, psychic hotlines, etc.)? Why do you think that God forbids his people to seek the future through the agency of mediums or psychics?

10. In spite of all that we hear in the news, why may Christians regard the future as bright?

Chapter 2:
'The First Coming of the Lord'
Pages 12-32

1. The Old Testament's teaching about the future centres on what historical events?

2. How does the Old Testament reveal the three-fold office of the coming Messiah?

3. What key element did the tabernacle reveal about the coming Messiah?

4. What is one of the most powerful and dramatic prophecies regarding the establishment of the kingdom of God?

5. Who will be included in the restoration of the people of God?

6. In what two ways does the Old Testament describe the 'day of the Lord' and of what two elements will it consist?

7. How do the perspectives upon the future of Old Testament and New Testament believers differ?

8. How has the kingdom already come?

9. What key event must take place in order for the kingdom to come to fulfilment?

10. What two events evidence the believer's blessings of salvation and serve as pledges for the future?

11. Why is it significant that Matthew 1:1ff. makes an appeal to the history of the Old Testament?

12. Why is the Old Testament's outlook on the future important for how we view the future?

13. Why is Genesis 3:15 called the 'Mother Promise' in the history of redemption?

14. How does the OT anticipate the ultimate establishment of God's kingdom? What other events foretold in the OT mark the inauguration of the latter days?

15. How does the Christian live 'between the times'?

16. What is the significance for the future of Christ's coming in the New Testament?

PART TWO:
THE FUTURE BETWEEN
DEATH AND RESURRECTION

CHAPTER 3:
'THE INTERMEDIATE STATE'
PAGES 35-75

1. What does the word 'eschatology' mean? Into what two parts is teaching about the future normally divided? What topics are covered in 'individual eschatology'?

2. Is death a 'natural' part of life? Why or why not? Reflect on Romans 5:12-21 and 1 Corinthians 15:26.

3. Since Christ has suffered the full wrath of God toward us on the cross, why do we as believers still have to die? Reflect on *Heidelberg Catechism* Question 42 (p. 38).

4. What is meant by the 'intermediate state'? List and briefly define two unbiblical views of the intermediate state.

5. What arguments are given in favour of the annihilationist view? Why do we reject this view?

6. What arguments are put forward in favour of 'soul sleep'? Why do we reject soul sleep?

7. What two biblical truths can be threatened by speaking about the 'immortality of the soul'? What would be a better term? For what reason? How should we best understand biblically the concept of the immortality of the soul?

8. What is progressive revelation and what is its significance with regard to the Old Testament teachings about the intermediate state? Defend the position that the Old Testament teaches the continuing conscious existence of the soul after death.

9. How does the New Testament reveal that believers and unbelievers continue to experience a conscious existence after death?

10. How does the New Testament contrast the intermediate state of believers with that of unbelievers? Which two New Testament texts explicitly affirm an intermediate state?

11. What does the Roman Catholic Church teach regarding purgatory and when did this dogma take full shape? What is the basis for this dogma? Why is the dogma of Purgatory fundamentally unchristian?

12. At the graveside, what is the believer's comfort?

PART THREE:
THE FUTURE OF CHRIST

CHAPTER 4:
'THE SECOND COMING OF CHRIST'
PAGES 79-109

1. What three terms are commonly used to describe the nature of Christ's return? What do these terms mean? What is the difference between them, if any?

2. Identify five features of the biblical understanding of Christ's return?

3. What viewpoints share the belief that Christ's return will occur in history, but will not conclude present history?

4. Why is it inappropriate to attempt to date Christ's return? What can we say about the time of Christ's Second Advent?

5. What do the Scriptures teach about the nature of Christ's return?

6. Reflect on 2 Thessalonians 1:17. How does this verse shape the character of Christian hope?

7. Prove from Scripture that Christ's Second Coming is a consummating event in history.

PART FOUR:
THE FUTURE MARKED BY
THE 'SIGNS OF THE TIMES'

CHAPTER 5:
'SIGNS OF GOD'S GRACE'
PAGES 113-139

1. How is the phrase 'signs of the times' used in the Scriptures? What does the phrase 'the signs of the times' refer to in Matthew 16:1?

2. What are three mistaken views regarding the 'signs of the times'?

3. Why can't the 'signs of the times' aid us in dating the return of Christ?

4. Into what three categories can the 'signs of the times' be organized? Which signs fall into each category?

5. How does the Old Testament anticipate the universal preaching of the gospel? How do Genesis 1-3 and the teaching of man as God's image-bearer anticipate the promise that the gospel will be preached to all peoples?

6. Read Psalm 22 and Isaiah 60:1-3. How is the salvation of the Gentiles inseparably joined to God's promise of salvation to his people Israel?

7. Reflect on how our confession of Christ's authority in ruling and reigning at the right hand of the Father relates to the preaching of the gospel to all the nations. Read Matthew 28:18-20 and Matthew 16:18. How does this guard against an 'unbiblical and distorted' view of the 'signs of the times'?

8. Read Romans 8:28-39. What is Paul's general solution to the problem that Romans 8:28-39 and Israel's rejection of Christ causes? How does Paul reconcile the falling away of God's chosen people with the promise that nothing will separate us from the love of God in Christ?

9. Does Israel's apostasy mean that God has rejected his chosen people? Why or why not?

10. What is Paul's specific solution to the problem of Israel's apostasy? How will God reconcile Israel to himself in the latter days? Where are we taught this in Scripture?

11. What are the three views regarding an understanding of 'all Israel' in Romans 11:26, and which is the best understanding of the phrase? What was the Old Testament promise regarding Israel? Has that promise failed? Why or why not?

12. Why would Paul's point in Romans 11:25 be undermined were we to understand the 'all Israel' of Romans 11:26 to be a reference only to the total number of the elect people of Israel, who make up only a remnant throughout the history of redemption?

13. Explain how the end-times events of Christ's Ascension and the outpouring of the Spirit on Pentecost are related to Matthew 24:14. Also reflect upon Joel 2:28-9, Acts 1:8, and 2:39.

14. What factors lead Christians to lose confidence in the power and importance of gospel preaching as opposed to other means of advancing the kingdom? Evaluate these alternative methods in light of Matthew 28:18-20.

15. What do we mean by a 'two-covenant theology'? How does Paul's argument in Romans 9-11 oppose a two-covenant position?

Chapter 6:
'Signs of Opposition and Judgment — 1'
Pages 140-158

1. What is the common circumstance of believers in the present period of history?

2. What is the 'preterist' view concerning Christ's words in the Olivet Discourse? What are some of the reasons for considering a secondary and more remote reference to Christ's words?

3. What biblical grounds do we have for saying that the prophesies of Matthew 24 have an initial fulfilment (i.e. to this generation) which foreshadows or anticipates a subsequent fulfilment prior to the return of Christ at the end of the age? Can you give examples of other prophecies in Scripture that have this characteristic of multiple fulfilments?

4. Why should Matthew 24 and 25 be treated as a unity?

5. How do most postmillennialists typically regard Matthew 24's reference to a 'great tribulation'? How should we understand the term 'the great tribulation' and the experience of believers in relation to it?

6. Why do you think that the conflict between the kingdom of God and the kingdom of the world will only intensify as Christ's return draws nearer?

7. How can tribulation nurture hope?

8. If tribulation characterizes the life of the kingdom-seeking-believer, what does it mean that the believer has peace? What is the nature of this peace? Read and reflect on 2 Timothy 3:12 and John 16:33.

9. How is the Second Coming of Christ characteristically described in the New Testament? See Matthew 24:29-21, 16:27, Mark 8:38, Acts 1:9-11, 1 Corinthians 15:52, 1 Thessalonians 4:16-17, 2 Thessalonians 1:7, and Revelation 1:7.

10. How are we to understand Paul's words in Colossians 1:24? What is meant by the phrase 'what is lacking in Christ's afflictions'?

11. What does Revelation 12:7-12 teach us about the certainty of Christ's victory in the midst of tribulation?

12. Why does persecution occasion perseverance and a hope of victory in the heart of the believer? Reflect on Romans 5:3-5 (also James 1:2-4).

13. Identify three metaphors that the Bible employs to describe God's purposes in bringing the believer through various trials and tribulations.

14. What biblical reasons do we have for rejecting the idea of a pre-tribulational rapture which snatches away the church just prior to the Great Tribulation?

CHAPTER 7:
'SIGNS OF OPPOSITION AND JUDGMENT—2'
PAGES 159-186

1. How does apostasy differ from other signs of the times? What characterizes what we call 'apostasy'? Reflect on Matthew 24:10-12, 1 Timothy 4:1, & 2 Timothy 3:1-9.

2. What are the consequences of apostasy for the church of Christ?

3. Is apostasy different from what is often called backsliding? What is the fundamental difference, if there is any?

4. Read 2 Thessalonians 2.
    (a.) Why does the enemy from within pose a greater danger to the church than all of the enemies that attack the church from without?
    (b.) Further reflect on Acts 20:25-31, 2 Peter 2:1-3 and 1 Timothy 4:1-5. How are false teachers described? What characterizes the teaching of these teachers? How do these teachers obscure or deny the gospel of the Lord Jesus Christ?

5. Does 2 Peter 1:5-11 give the church an antidote against apostasy?

6. In what ways is the church today liable to apostasy? What should be the believer's attitude toward the possibility of such apostasy? Read 2 Peter 3:17-18 and Revelation 2:5.

7. What ways do the sins of smugness and self-satisfaction lead to complacency? How could this presumption make the church liable to apostasy?

8. Why can't the church catholic ever fall away? Provide a scriptural warrant for this confession (cf. *Belgic Confession*, Article 27).

9. Read 2 Thessalonians 2:15. How must the church fortify herself against the temptation to fall away from the living God?

10. What are some observations that can be made regarding biblical teaching on the 'man of lawlessness' or 'the Antichrist'? What most characterizes the spirit of Antichrist? Why could a liberal theologian who denies the bodily resurrection of Christ more plausibly be regarded as antichrist than a notorious political figure like Hitler?

11. What reasons might lead us to conclude that 'the Antichrist' is a specific historical person who is revealed prior to the return of Jesus Christ? Cf. 2 Thessalonians 2 and 1 John 2:18.

12. What Old Testament passages provide the background for Christ's prediction of wars and rumours of wars, earthquakes, famine and pestilence? What does this teach us about these signs in general? What is the pattern in history concerning signs such as wars and rumours of wars, earthquakes, pestilence and famine?

13. Where in the Bible and in what context is the only specific mention of the Battle of Armageddon? What grand theme does the Battle of Armageddon confirm? Do you think that Revelation 17:14, 19:19 and 20:8 refer to the battle of Armageddon? How are we to understand these passages?

14. What Old Testament prophecies speak of a great and final conflict between the Lord and his enemies? What significance can we draw between the battle between Israel and the Canaanite King, Jabin, and the battle of Armageddon in Revelation 16 (cf. Judges 5)?

15. What hope can the church derive from the Bible's teaching of a great and final battle between the Lord and his enemies (i.e. the battle of Armageddon)? Reflect on this in connection with Psalm 2.

PART FIVE:
THE FUTURE OF THE KINGDOM

CHAPTER 8:
'PREMILLENNIAL VIEWS'
PAGES 189-218

1. What is the meaning of the term 'millennium'? How is 'Chiliasm' more narrowly defined?

2. What are the two major types of millennial positions and the two prominent versions of each?

3. What are the primary features of historic premillennialism?

4. Which view is relatively new in history and what is its primary feature?

5. What is an even more recent development in this view and how does it differ from older versions?

6. What prominent themes have emerged from our study thus far which intersect with our treatment of the millennium?

7. How does our argument that the return of Christ is a consummating event argue against the Premillennial view of a thousand year reign of Christ?

8. Who were the Montanists and what did they teach?

9. Why is Historic Premillennialism often referred to as 'post-tribulationism'?

10. What are the two important biblical texts to which Historic Premillennialists appeal for their two-resurrection position?

11. What are the three stages of history identified by premillennialists?

12. Name at least three modern adherents/propounders of Dispensational Premillennialism.

13. Define the term 'Dispensationalism' or 'dispensation'. How many dispensations are commonly distinguished among dispensationalists? Identify them.

14. What is the place of the church with respect to Israel in Dispensational Premillennialism?

15. What kind of a hermeneutic does Dispensational Premillennialism employ?

16. To what dispensation do the Old Testament prophecies concerning the nation of Israel refer? When will the church dispensation conclude?

17. What are the main characteristics of the Dispensational Premillennialism view of the millennial kingdom?

18. What features distinguish Dispensational Premillennialism from Historic Premillennialism?

CHAPTER 9:
'POSTMILLENNIAL VIEWS'
PAGES 219-243

1. What general feature distinguishes all postmillennial views?

2. What developments have occurred in the twentieth century with regard to postmillennialism?

3. What is the problem with the term 'Amillennial'? Why was it coined? If the term 'Amillennialism' literally means 'no millennium', how can it be included among the three other major millennial views?

4. How long has the Amillennial view been present in church history, and who was instrumental in establishing this view?

5. What is the predominant view among Reformed churches in the world today?

6. What are some distinctive features of Amillennialism?

7. What is the fundamental difference between pre- and post-millennial views?

8. What are the basic features of 'Christian Reconstructionism'?

9. What is Postmillennialism's biblical warrant for the promise of a universal covenant blessing?

10. How do Postmillennialists apply Psalm 2, Isaiah 2:2-4 and 1 Corinthians 15:25?

11. How do preterists interpret the 'signs of the times'?

12. What is the postmillennial understanding of Revelation 20?

13. How does Amillennialism conceive of the millennium?

14. How does Amillennialism understand the 'signs of the times'?

15. What is Amillennialism's teaching on Revelation 20?

16. What is Amillennialism's 'hope for the future' and how does this differ from Postmillennialism?

Chapter 10:
'Evaluating Premillennialism'
Pages 244-295

1. What two-phase view predominates in premillennialism, and what are the phases? Does biblical teaching support the two-phase view? Why or why not?

2. How do premillennialists view the new covenant church? How should the new covenant church be viewed with regard to the people of God in the old covenant?

3. What are some of the problems with the idea that God has postponed his dealings with Israel?

4. Who belongs to 'the Israel of God'?

5. In what manner do dispensationalists read the Bible, and what is their related criticism of other views?

6. What are the two problems with the dispensationalist way of reading the Bible?

7. How did the Reformers advocate reading the Bible?

8. What are three problem areas of dispensational understanding?

9. Give three reasons why the general teaching of Scripture disproves the Premillennial view? Give Scripture references.

10. Read 1 Corinthians 15:23-26 and answer the following questions:
    (a.) What is Ladd's argument for the premillennial view of the millennium?
    (b.) Is this view possible?
    (c.) What reasons are offered against his view?

11. What are the distinctives of pre-tribulational rapturism?

12. What indication do we have from the Olivet Discourse that believers will not be 'raptured' before the tribulation described by Christ?

13. Why do dispensationalists argue that the elect mentioned by Jesus in Matthew 24 refers only to the Jews and not to Gentile believers?

14. Read 1 Thessalonians 4:13-18. Why can't dispensationalists sustain an argument for the rapture from these verses?

15. Read Hebrews 12:22-23. What do these verses teach us about the church in God's plan in history?

16. What are some New Testament epithets for the church and what are their Old Testament significance?

17. What passages in Scripture teach that the church is the 'central accomplishment and interest of the Lord Jesus in history'?

18. How does Romans 11:25 make it unmistakably clear that the people of God are one and not two?

19. Discuss certain inherent problems with the hermeneutic of literalism.

20. Can you think of any examples where dispensationalists treat the text in a non-literal way? What do you think this means for their interpretive method?

21. According to dispensationalists, why can't the promises made to Israel in the Old Testament be applied to the church?

22. Read 1 Corinthians 1:20 and analyze the claim that the promises of the Old Testament made to Israel cannot be applied to the church.

23. Why is typology a problem for dispensationalists?

CHAPTER 11:
'WHAT ABOUT REVELATION 20?'
PAGES 296-339

1. What is the starting point for the Premillennial understanding of Revelation 20? How should the chronology of the events described in Revelation 19 and 20 be understood? Describe the relationship that dispensationalists posit between Revelation chapter 19 and 20. For those who assert that the millennium is now, how do they explain the relationship between Revelation 19:11-21 and 20:1-11?

2. Explain and illustrate the 'recapitulatory structure' of the book of Revelation.

3. What reasons are adduced for Revelation 20 describing the period between the first and second comings of Christ?

4. How are we to understand 'the binding of Satan'? How do premillennialists understand 'the binding of Satan'? What role does the 'binding of Satan' have in the Premillennialist vision of the end times? Given the Premillennial view of the binding of Satan during the millennium, why would dispensationalists reject the Amillennial view that this present age constitutes the millennium?

5. How should we understand the binding of Satan in the present age? Demonstrate how this is demonstrated in the ministry of Jesus Christ in the Gospels.

6. How are we to understand 'a thousand years'? What are some problems with the Premillennialist view that the millennium is a literal 1,000 years? Give some biblical examples where the number 1000 is used symbolically.

7. Who are the saints depicted in Revelation 20:4-6 and where are they? What is the likeliest location for John's vision in Revelation 20:4-6? Why?

8. What is the Premillennial view regarding the resurrections of Revelation 20?

9. How are we to understand 'the first resurrection'? How does the reference to the 'the rest of the dead' in this passage support the view that the 'first resurrection' mentioned here is not a physical resurrection? How do premillennialists understand the first resurrection of Revelation 20:4-6?

10. What Scriptural considerations lead us to regard the first resurrection as a spiritual participation in Christ as well as immunity from the second death?

Chapter 12:
'Evaluating Postmillennialism'
Pages 340-360

1. What is the view of 'Golden-Age' Postmillennialism? What is the broad meaning of postmillennial?

2. What are some biblical arguments against 'Golden-Age' Postmillennialism?

3. Why does 'Golden-Age' Postmillennialism diminish the believer's hope for the future?

4. Are the Reformed confessions incompatible with Postmillennialism?

5. What frame of mind is exhibited in Amillennialism?

6. Read both Philippians 2:9-11 and Ephesians 1:22-23, and explain in what way these passages argue against 'Golden-Age' Postmillennialism.

7. Give reasons why 1 Corinthians 15:22-26 does not argue in favour of 'Golden-Age' Postmillennialism.

8. What Scriptures lead us to conclude that the 'signs of the times' will characterize life in this present age until the

second coming of Christ? What significance does this have for an evaluation of 'Golden-Age' Postmillennialism?

9. How does 'Golden-Age' Postmillennialism mute the biblical teaching of fellowship in the suffering of Christ? Is this view triumphalistic? Explain.

10. Read Romans 9:28 and Titus 2:13. What is the believer's hope in this life, and does 'Golden-Age' Postmillennialism alter that focus?

11. Evaluate the Postmillennialist claim that Amillennialism is 'pessimistic'. What do you think of the term 'optimistic Amillennialism'?

PART SIX:
THE FUTURE OF
ALL THINGS

CHAPTER 13:
'THE RESURRECTION OF THE BODY'
PAGES 363-391

1. What do we mean by 'concomitants of the second advent'?

2. How many resurrections will occur? On what basis do we reject the Premillennial teaching of two resurrections? Read 1 Corinthians 15:23-24 and explain why this passage does not support a two-resurrection theology.

3. What is the significance of the seed metaphor for the resurrection of the body?

4. What is the distinction between the natural body and the resurrection body? What is the relation of the resurrection body to Christ?

5. How is the resurrection of the body linked to the renewal of creation?

6. Who raises the dead on the last day? Why is this an important question?

7. Reflect on 2 Corinthians 5:1-9. What does this passage teach us about the nature of the resurrection? Does 2 Corinthians 5:1-9 teach that believers will receive an interim resurrection body between death and resurrection?

8. On what basis do we reject the teaching that the resurrection body will be non-material or made of spiritual stuff versus material stuff? What arguments are put forward against the teaching that our resurrection body will be immaterial?

9. Why is the statement 'this is not your loved one' a misguided way to speak of the deceased?

10. Why have Christians historically avoided cremation? What does the *Westminster Larger Catechism* Q&A 86 have to say about cremation?

11. Does Matthew 22:30 teach that we will not recognize each other in the resurrection?

12. What will become of bodies that have been utterly annihilated?

13. What does the Bible teach us about unborn children or infants who die in infancy? Will they participate in the resurrection?

14. What can we say about the resurrection of those who were born with severe physical or mental impairments?

Chapter 14:
'The Final Judgment'
Pages 392-419

1. Will the final judgment of unbelievers be an investigation or an indictment?

2. Who will be judged? Will believers also be judged in the judgment at the last day? If so, what will this judgment consist of?

3. Who will be the judge at the judgment? What about 1 Corinthians 6:2-3 (or Matthew 19:28)?

4. What will be judged? According to what standard?

5. Why do we reject the Premillennial view that there will be various judgments before and after the millennium?

6. What indications do we have that the judgment will occur after the general renewal of all things?

7. Why is the final judgment necessary for those who have died prior to the return of Christ?

8. Read Romans 1:18-23. Reflect on what happens to those who did not have an opportunity to hear the gospel.

9. Are there gradations of reward or punishment in the judgment? Will there be degrees of reward in heaven? Is the idea of degrees of reward inconsistent with the gospel? In other words, do believers merit or earn their rewards? Consider Luke 17:7-10. How can such an idea be consistent with the concept of unmerited grace?

10. Is reward a proper motivation to Christian obedience? Why or why not?

11. Is the idea of reward incompatible with the perfect blessedness of the final state?

12. What is the difference between condign and congruent merit in the teaching of the Roman Catholic Church?

CHAPTER 15:
'THE DOCTRINE OF ETERNAL PUNISHMENT'
PAGES 420-453

1. What is hell? What are two common alternatives being proposed today?

2. What is conditional immortality?

3. What three main (biblical) objections do advocates of conditional immortality advance against the doctrine of hell? What Scriptures do they use in support of their position?

4. Why does theologian Clark Pinnock abhor the idea of hell? What does the popular version of his view sound like?

5. Why do advocates of conditional immortality say that hell is incompatible with God's justice?

6. How many meanings can be assigned to the word commonly translated 'to destroy' in the Scripture? What implication does this have for the arguments of the conditional immortality advocates?

7. What do annihilationists fail to take seriously about the language of a 'consuming fire'? Why is this a problem?

8. What metaphors are used to describe hell in the Bible? How should we interpret the meaning of this symbolic language? What contradictions among the descriptions of hell lead us to read these figures as metaphors?

9. Reflect on the implication that Matthew 26:46 has on the annihilationist view that the wicked cease to exist after experiencing God's judgment. Also reflect on Revelation 14:10-11.

10. Does the doctrine of hell contradict the biblical teaching about the love of God? Why or why not?

11. Is the concept of eternal punishment incompatible with the righteousness of God's justice? Why or why not? In what ways are we tempted to impose (inadvertently?) our modern notions of retribution and punishment upon the biblical revelation of hell? How can God be both just and merciful to sinners who violate his law?

12. How was Christ's atonement properly a vindication of God's justice? Reflect on Romans 3:21-26.

13. How will sinners in hell view God? Evaluate the claim that the ungodly continue to sin and rebel against God even in hell? Consider Revelation 22:10-11 and 16:21. What conclusions can we draw from these passages?

14. Does hell represent a failure or limitation of God's redemptive work in Christ? Does hell make the final state less than perfectly glorious? Does Revelation 22:5 support this claim?

15. What are the basic tenets of Universalism?

CHAPTER 16:
'THE NEW HEAVENS AND NEW EARTH'
PAGES 454-488

1. In what three ways is the term 'heaven' commonly used in the Scriptures? Give references.

2. Why is it significant that the new creation will embrace heaven and earth?

3. How will the new creation differ from the first? Will there be a new creation or will this creation be made new? What continuity and discontinuity will there be between the present 'heaven and earth' and the New Creation? What is the difference between seeing the life to come as a repristination versus a restoration of all things?

4. Why would it constitute a 'great victory' for Satan if God had to annihilate the present creation to remake or renew it?

5. What has been the effect of sin on 'heaven and earth' and how does Christ's work of redemption remedy that problem? Consider Ephesians 1:10 and 2 Peter 3:13. Explain the relationship between 2 Peter 3:5-13 and Romans 8?

6. Read 2 Peter 3:5-13. Do the details of this passage support the suggestion that the present order will be annihilated? What the does the imagery of fire represent? What does the expression in 2 Peter 3:10, 'and the earth and its works will be discovered' suggest about the New Creation?

7. Why is it so difficult for us to describe or imagine heaven? In what way can it be said that the believer already knows something experientially of the final state of glory (cf. *1 Cor.* 13:12)? What aspects of our present experience cloud that reality?

8. What are some blessings of the life to come for the people of God?

9. What will be the primary aspect of life in the new heavens and earth? In what way is the Lord's Day but a foretaste of the life to come? What is the deepest longing of every image-bearer of God? Reflect on *Westminster Shorter Catechism* Q&A 1, Psalm 73:25 and 42:1-2.

10. Will we work or rest in heaven? Explain. Won't we get bored in the life to come that never ends? Why or why not? Support your answer with Scripture.

11. What are some things that will contribute to the glory and richness of heaven? What indication do we have that we will continue to experience the diversity of human

life and culture? What implications does our answer to this question have?

12. What will seeing God 'face to face' mean in heaven?

13. Reflect on the implications of Revelation 21:1-4 for life in the New Creation.

14. In what way has sin affected our ability to both glorify and enjoy God? How does the work of Christ repair this relationship? Reflect on Romans 8:1 and 1 Corinthians 1:30.

15. How does Revelation 22:1-5 describe our enjoyment and communion with God in the life to come?

16. In what way, according to Wolters, are we made 'partakers of the divine nature'? How does this differ from the Eastern Orthodox doctrine of theosis?

*Other books by Cornelis P. Venema
published by the Trust*

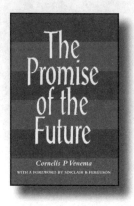
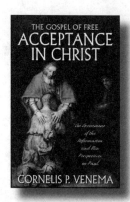
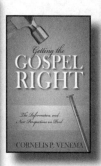
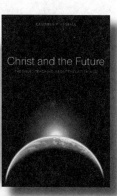